THE **100** BEST **FOREPLAY** **TIPS** EVER!

THIS IS A CARLTON BOOK

Text and design copyright © Carlton Books Limited 2007

This edition published by
Carlton Books Limited 2007
20 Mortimer Street
London W1T 3JW

A CIP catalogue record for this book is available from the British Library.

UK ISBN 978 1 84442 071 1
US ISBN 978 1 84732 016 2

Reprinted in 2008.
Printed and bound in China

Executive Editor: Lisa Dyer
Senior Art Editor: Gülen Shevki-Taylor
Design: Anna Knight
Production: Fifi von Trapp

# THE 100 BEST
# FOREPLAY
# TIPS
# EVER!

**LISA SUSSMAN**

**CARLTON**
BOOKS

# Section One

# Warm-up Moves

Foreplay isn't just a little pre-entertainment before the main event. It's what puts the "oh, ohh, ohhh"! in your big O's. You get more blood flowing from the extremities of the body toward the parts that need them and a heightened sensitivity all over. Get enough of the stuff and even a light caress on your wrist can make you throb.

**One problem:** Because your average guy is basically good to go from the moment he wakes up in the morning, it's thought that foreplay is a special little something he does for you. Not so. A recent study proves that guys ache for a little pre-sex action. However, because his body has a different setup (notice the penis?), many women really don't know the little touches that get his pulse pounding. Read on for how you can both get the bedroom build-up you crave.

# Must-do Smooches

Nine dishy, gotta-have-it-now lip locks to lay on each other right now. Pucker up!

**1** Alternate between deep teeth-gnashing, lip-bruising French kisses (for him) and light, feathery kisses (for her).

# 2

Don't just go mouth-to-mouth. Throw your whole body into it. Cradle his face with one hand and grab his bottom with the other while grinding your breasts and pelvis against him.

**3** Master this tongue teaser: While making out, wrap your lips around his tongue and suck, starting slow and soft and gradually building up to fast and stiff. It'll feel like you're making love to his mouth.

**4** Kiss each other some sweet place you never have before.

**5** Pack a more powerful erotic punch by not-quite kissing him. Hover above him, gliding your lips over his, but pulling back the second he tries to connect. Repeat a few times before going in for a deep smooch.

Time yourselves. Kissing for at least 20 seconds twice a day (the average relationship lip-greets only ten seconds a day max) will keep your passion motors in overdrive all day.

7

According to Tantric text, a woman's upper lip has an energy channel that connects with her clitoris. When kissed just right, it can start a sexual bonfire that burns through both your bodies. To spark things, he should kiss your upper lip while you kiss his lower lip (FYI, reversing this arrangement has a cold-water effect).

Men like their foreplay hard and heavy. So make him
drool with these five lip-licking smack downs.

- Tug his bottom lip with your teeth

- Lightly suck his tongue when it's in your mouth

- Nibble at his neck

- Tickle the roof of his mouth with your tongue

- Cup his head and pull him toward you
  to deepen the kiss.

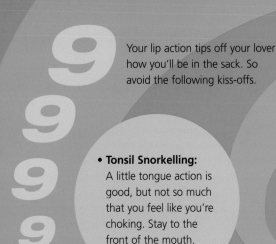

Your lip action tips off your lover how you'll be in the sack. So avoid the following kiss-offs.

- **Tonsil Snorkelling:**
  A little tongue action is good, but not so much that you feel like you're choking. Stay to the front of the mouth.

- **Sucking Face:** It's called snogging, not noshing. Swallow to keep your saliva at a juicy but manageable level.

- **Being Steadfast:** Good for commitment, but not such a hot kissing trait. Keep moving using different motions and amounts of pressure – slide your lips over each other's faces, use your tongue to dart and swirl, and keep your hands moving.

- **Peckers:** Unless it's a quickie, plan on more than just 30 seconds of continuous bussing to really heat things up.

# Five Instant Turn-ons

Tips that will get you both in the mood to – ahem – get in the mood. Surprise – you'll be fully clothed!

## 10

Talk the talk. Memorize the following phrases and use at your own carnal risk.

- Caress your lover's cheek, lock eyes and utter three simple words: **"I want you"**.

- Any email longer than **"CU Later"** will keep you on each other's brains all day and make it easier to slip into some one-on-one action when you are F2F.

- Scream, **"Boo"**. Scaring each other stimulates the neurotransmitter dopamine in the brain, which can trigger your sex drive.

- **Give a compliment.** It will make your lover feel noticed, special and appreciated, and closer to you… all of which add up to him feeling more inclined to make you feel good in bed.

- Saying **"I don't need to answer that"** if your mobile or pager goes off while you're together guarantees an orgasm later.

Caress the tresses. Each hair follicle has its own sensitive nerve. Sink your fingers in, lightly pull the shafts up and away from the scalp and they'll feel it right down to their curling toes.

Pick up a pair of furry handcuffs (available from sex shops like **www.annsummers.com, www.libida.com and www.sh-womenstore.com)** and pass them to him under the table at a restaurant, saying "Here's a little something for later." He'll be asking for the bill before you finish your sentence.

12

Work from the bottom. Take turns **massaging** the length of each other's legs, from the **upper thighs** down to the **ankles**. Then focus on the **feet**, kneading the **heels** and all other points beneath. Last of all, zero in on the **toes**, stretching and sucking them individually.

13

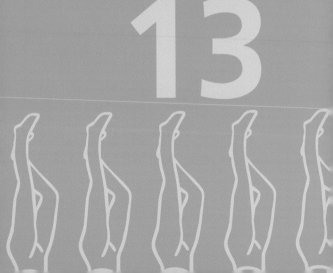

# 14

Cooking together heats up more than the kitchen. Whip up an easy sophisticated cheesy snack (sauté asparagus stalks in olive oil for three minutes, sprinkle with Parmesan, salt and pepper) that's packed with zinc, a key mineral needed for getting and **staying lusty**. Add a clove of crushed garlic if you want to boost blood flow to special places. Follow with a wicked chocolate dessert and you'll load up on phenylethylamine, a neurotransmitter that activates the brain's pleasure centre, and caffeine, which can jolt your **sex drive**. Start feasting.

Never underestimate
the heating power of
a great big bear hug.

**16**

Put on lipstick in front of him.
He'll start fantasizing about your
lips and what he wants them to
do. Better yet, let him put it on
your lips for you.

# Fair Play

His 'n' her get-busy-in-a-jiffy basics that'll deliver mind-blowing results.

**17**

Yes, you could just speed ahead to grabbing his penis and pulling to turn him on. But it's so much more fun for him (and you) to dawdle and diddle in the slow lane. Here are five slow-mo moves that might get him arrested for sexually loitering.

- Get him to take a deep breath. Whatever activity he's attempting (World Championship Ironman or your own personal iron man), deep, regulated breathing will help him stay in control without losing his will. When he feels like he's burning out, he should stay very still, relax his genital muscles, and take a long breath in through his nose for a count of five seconds and hold it for two before slowly exhaling through his mouth for six seconds. He'll be able to stay in peak condition for as long as you want to play.

- Go ahead and bring him to the brink. Then ignore him. It's a guaranteed way to send him into a frenzy... and swell his orgasm later.

- Trick him. Get this close to his naughty bits with your mouth and then pass right on by. To really make him twist and burn, blast some hot air into the area.

- Indulge your inner dominatrix. Position his body how you want it or, if he makes a move to head down below, pull him back up if you're not ready. Being the object of your sexual attention will bring his entire body to a fever pitch. He doesn't have to ask for what he wants or worry about how he's doing performance-wise. And playing Mistress means you get the kind of stimulation you need, when and where you want it.

- Don't forget: You have a whole body there – not just 6 in (15.2 cm). Spend at least an hour tracing the outlines of his frame with your fingertips without saying a word.

You can only speed things up so much. Study after study shows that women need at least 15 minutes of foreplay before they're good and ready to move on both mentally and physically (in addition to having do-me-now urges, she needs to start lubricating and her vaginal canal must expand to handle his – er – abundance). These five moves will rev your engine. Don't be shy – most men are willing and eager to do whatever it takes to please their bedfellow.

- Pick up some female-friendly porn like the *Black Lace* or *X Libris* series to read together. Besides getting you hot under the collar, the torrid prose will give him lots of sizzling ideas for bawdy things he can try with you.

- He can send you into a tailspin simply by spiralling his fingertips along your forearms, neck, the palms of your hands and any other sensitive body spot. The circular motion is much more intense than the usual up-and-down straight line rub.

- Don't beat around the bush about requesting oral. It's the shortest, fastest route to paradise for most women (a fluent cunnilinguist can bring a woman to orgasm in minutes).

- When in doubt, kiss. Women get immense erotic pleasure from frequent, lusty, passionate make-out sessions. Just remember that this does not always mean frantically wrestling tongues. Try to mix up your lip play with the occasional oh-so-seductive butterfly peck on the nose, eyes, forehead and other body parts.

- For a heart-racing sensation, have him almost-caress you by holding his fingertips just above your skin and running his hands over your naked arms, breasts, belly and thighs so they just brush those fine body hairs. Mmmm.

## Section Two

# Lose Your Senses

Too often, touch is the only sense that takes centre stage when you're doing the passion rumba. But bringing all of your senses into the experience will transform your foreplay from nice-but-basic to a full mind-body, haul-out-the-fireworks fantasia.

Every type of sensory stimulation, from the sight of your lover's naked body to the sound of their voice whispering in your ear to the potent smell and taste of their skin turns on parts of the brain responsible for getting your buzz on. Read on for the tantalizing secrets that'll make you feel like the ultimate sensual seductress. You can use these tips to focus on one sense at a time or create a combo platter that treats several senses at once. Don't expect to be of sound mind once you're finished.

Surround yourself with these sexy sounds…

• Say something. Anything. Even if it's "Uhhhh". If you're not up to expressing your own pleasure, a bare-bones string of four-word phrases whispered in the heat of the moment can work wonders. Try, "Do you like that?" or "Does that feel good?"

• So you want a little foul-mouthed foreplay? Good. But it's only sexy talk if you're speaking the same language. Sit opposite each other, point to your bits and decide together what you're going to call them. Clothing optional.

• You don't have to have a dirty dialogue to make things hot. Just breathing each other's names every once in a while between the "Yeahs" and "Ooh, babys" here or there is proof that you're what's making your lover feel so good (and that you remember who you're in bed with).

- When it comes to making sheet music together, some tunes rap out a sexier beat than others. Any number that has you toe-tapping faster than the human heartbeat (about 72 RPMs) will arouse your doin'-it desires while slow-beat scores like those found in reggae, Latin or Barry White songs will send good vibrations throbbing through your lower body.

- Talk in public. Plant yourself in a crowded place (on a blanket in a park, at a club or party, in a busy restaurant) and whisper your fantasies to one another, sparing no racy detail. You can do something about it later, when you get home.

- Let the foreplay begin on your drive home. Call your lover and say you've been thinking all day about having a passionate, steamy encounter with them. Or tell them you'll meet them at a specific time in the bedroom with no clothes on.

# 20

Savour these tasty treats…

- Before tongue diving between their legs, swish with a minty mouthwash for 30 seconds. It will make your tongue feel tingly good on their nether regions and make them taste fresh as a stick of gum.

- Order the tasting menu. There are so many yummy flavours of lubricant and edible body products (see tips 12 and 68 for resources) now available, why settle for just one? Dab different flavours of lubricant strategically over your different erogenous zones and have your sweetie nibble your skin to discover them one by one. They'll soon be searching your body for more!

- What you eat can make a big difference to your pre-blow-out action. Here, a hungry girl's guide to working some food into your foreplay.

Drizzle each other with champagne and lick it off as it fizzes on your skin.

A sprinkle of cinnamon down there will wake him up like morning coffee.

On a hot night, lick the salt off each other's sweaty bodies.

Hunt the sweet spot. Dab a little honey or chocolate syrup on your body and then challenge your lover to find it using only their tongue.

Get juicy by rubbing a sticky fruit like papaya or mango all over each others' bodies and then licking each other clean.

Take a can of whipped cream to bed with you. Enjoy.

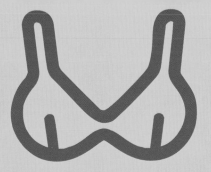

Use the following to put on your own
private peep show.

- You don't even need to touch him. Just seeing you do
  some sexy thing injects an instant shot of testosterone
  into his bloodstream. Put him on guard by locking
  eyes with him. Then reach under your shirt, arch and
  unclasp your bra. Wriggle it free and toss it toward
  him. He'll be all over you.

• Men like to see naked women. But if you don't feel comfortable putting on a strip show, have him undress you, slowly, and caressing and kissing each part of your body as it comes into view.

• Stay in the spotlight. Leave the lights on, light a few candles or get busy in the daylight hours.

• As you play, pull back your hair so he can see what's going on.

• Set the action in front of a mirror so you can both watch.

• Watch a skin flick with the sound off (it's actually much hotter when you lose the stilted horny workman-smutty housewife dialogue).

# 22

The nose is connected to the limbic system of the brain, which controls libido. Seduce it with these intoxicating scents.

- Certain floral aromas can trigger sexual arousal. Put a couple of drops of rose, jasmine and ylang-ylang oil on the light bulb in your bedside lamp, switch it on and get turned on.

- Spray a touch of his cologne on the sheets. One study found that women who fantasized while smelling a popular men's cologne were more aroused than when smelling women's cologne or a neutral odour. If he doesn't have a signature scent, shop for one with him. That's foreplay, too.

- Raid the pantry. Research shows that guys turn into lust-crazed beasts (or similar) at the smell of cinnamon buns, lavender, vanilla, doughnuts and pumpkin pie (interestingly, french fries and beer didn't make the list). Women also get off from sniffing lavender and pumpkin pie, as well as liquorice and cucumber.

- Perfuming your lower stomach is a much more effective aphrodisiac than spraying your wrists. As you become aroused, blood flows to the pelvis, generating heat and releasing the fragrance. Try something with spicy tones, which has been shown in studies to have a boosting effect on his penis.

- Skip the perfume altogether. One study found that men who sniffed vaginal secretions are more likely to find a woman attractive than men who took a whiff of water.

Thrill each other with these tantalizing touches.

• Take a steamy shower together... with the lights out.

• For extra shower power, make it a threesome: Pour a couple of drops of shower gel into a spray bottle and mix it with water. Spray each other, then rub. You'll feel three different types of stimulation – the steady pelting of the shower, the soft spray of the soapy gel and the firm caresses of your lover's mitts.

• There are parts of your body that are so seldom touched that they are, by default, especially sensitive. Discover yours by touching each other using any part of your body – your hair, your feet, your lips – except your hands.

23

- When it comes to foreplay, men and women crave distinctly different finger moves. Women get turned on by softer, gentler caresses while men typically want things hard and harder. Take turns giving each other a sensuous gender-customized stroking. He can use a feather to lightly trace tingly touches over your skin while you can limber up your hands with oil to give him a deep penetrating rubdown all over his body.

- Avoid these touchy-feely moves:

  Scratching anywhere near his boys with inch-long talons

  Rubbing him down with patchouli, rose, jasmine or any other girlie-scented oil

  Pinching, punching or anything that will leave bruises

  Jamming his boner so hard it cracks

  Tickling him until he pees in his pants.

## Section Three

# Feeling Feverish

Your skin is jam-packed with 45 miles (72 km) of sensitive nerves that are often ignored as you head toward your more guaranteed pleasure launch locations. But caressed the right way these oh-yeah zones will deliver a mega jolt to your sex play. (Yes, that goes for men, too. The male body is so much more than his little bobble-headed mate.)

Check out the tips in this section to find out how to travel beyond the usual hot spots to explore some erotic locations on your body that you probably won't find in your average sexual tour guide. Pack some massage oil and let the voyage of carnal discovery begin.

# Your Pleasure Map

Don't leave home base until you read this.

**24** When using your hands, keep them both in constant motion to maintain the experience at high-pitch.

**25** Instead of working your way through your bodies following your usual head-to-toe map, go off-road and jump from spot to spot, moving your fingers, lips, tongue and stick shift in erratic patterns instead of a straight line. Never knowing where you're going to touch next keeps every nerve he has constantly on the edge.

**26** Warning – some of these body parts don't often see the light of day so make sure they all pass the sniff test (places to wield a washcloth and soap: behind the ears, between the breasts, the belly button, underarms, the top crease of the bottom and the toes). According to one study, good grooming counts even higher than penis or breast size with some lovers!

Everyone has their own specific sequence of caresses that turns them from docile playmate to a sex maniac. Here's a no-hassle way to access each other's code: Lie together naked (sounds like fun already, doesn't it?) and take turns trying different touches on your bodies. Give each fondle a number between one and ten, depending on how good it feels. When you get really good at this, you can say, "Give me a number ten and make it snappy!"

Play in the zone. Getting as close to tried-and-trues without actually touching them will make you wiggle and wriggle for more. By the time you actually cross over their erogenous borders, the sensation will be that much more earth-shaking.

# Head Rush

Here are five heady touches to the noggin.

## 29

Firmly roll the edge of the ear between your forefinger, middle finger and thumb, going back and forth from lobe to top.

## 30

Find the pulse point (around 1¼ in / 3.5 cm under the earlobes and just under the jawbone) and, using three of your fingers, rub tiny circles with very light strokes. If you're doing it right, you should feel their pulse start moving faster than a train).

**31** To release endorphins and get your lover in the mood, use your tongue or finger to lightly probe the ultra-sensitive skin behind the ear.

**32** Stimulate the auriculogenital reflex (ear-stimulation response) by heavy breathing into the ear. Some people find it so exciting they actually climax from it.

**33** Give him an eye-opener by lavishing his lids with dry, light kisses. Finish by gently breathing hot air over his lashes.

# Go Neck-in-Neck

Try these five steamy ways to neck-it.

**34**

Give goosebumps by kissing the back of the neck very softly.

**35**

Devour, suck and nibble at the soft skin where the neck meets the jawline.

**36**

Men's neck skin tends to be thicker than yours, so use your whole mouth to suck on his skin. Or alternate sucking with gently biting a path up and down his neck.

If you want to leave your mark, suck in one spot hard. Ambidextrous vampires can use their tongues to caress and soothe the bruised skin at the same time.

37

Brush your lips between their throat and chin where the skin is thinner so the nerves and blood vessels are closer to the surface.

38

The skin on the inside of the elbows is chock-full of close-to-the-surface nerves. To make their body tingle, run your forefinger from the palm to the crease of the arm and linger there for a bit.

# 40

There are 40,000 nerve endings in each of the palms just waiting to be tickled, teased and tantalized. With your fingernails, lightly scratch small, gradually widening circles into the open palm until you're tracing the outer edges of his palm.

# 41

Run the pads of your fingertips up and down their outstretched fingers.

# 42

Flick your tongue quickly in and out of the centre of the palm.

**43** Give your lover shivers by licking their wrist and then blowing softly to create a cooling sensation – special receptors there are tuned to detect differences in temperature.

**44** Slowly, lightly stroking their hand from the palm up toward the fingertips will kick the area's touch receptors in gear and awaken other parts of their body.

**45** Gently suck on and lick their armpit.

# Middle Ground

Two luscious tactics for the treasure chest.

## 46

Anyone can maul breasts like a porn star, but it's the superstar lover who knows to trail a wet line between your breasts.

## 47

Meet chest to chest and press.

# Belly Love

Press the button with these two racy moves.

The area between the belly button and pubic bone is packed with pleasure points. To arouse them all, massage, lick or nibble the soft skin from the navel down to where the pubic hair begins.

**48**

Belly orgasm. Take turns sitting erect on the edge of a chair with the other person standing behind. The one standing places their hands in a triangle on the sitter's abdomen, pointing downward, and rubs. The person on the receiving end will soon feel a sexy buzz building up.

# Side-by-Side

No one is going to give you a red card for performing these two off-side penalties.

## 50

The skin from underneath the armpits to just above the hips is one long orgasmic runway. Take off using long, slow, continuous strokes with the palms of your open hands, circling at the hips and coming back up to where you started. If you're causing more giggles than sighs, then you're working too shallow and too quickly.

## 51

Gently tongue and nibble along the melt-down inner crease where the elbow meets the upper arm.

# Back-up

Get their back up with these three dishy strokes.

**52** Gently rubbing the base of the spine will send shivers up their back and way down below.

**53** The small dent just above the crease of the bottom (aka "the sacrum") is absolutely packed with sensitive nerve endings. Use your fingers to rub its surface and around its edges. The harder the better, so don't be afraid to put your whole body into it.

**54** As you get lower down the back, the nerves become more sensitive. Work the whole area by gently kneading the muscles between the shoulder blades and spine, and then immediately following up with light fingertip strokes.

# Leg-it

Master these three heavenly steps.

## 55

Because of its out-of-the way location, the back of the leg from the knee down to the ankle rarely gets touched. But the skin here is so thin that all it takes is a little continuous stroking to make your lover weak at the knees. Use the backs of your fingers and fingernails like a feather duster, delicately brushing the area with light up-and-down strokes. Avoid a tickling sensation by following up with a firmer touch to stimulate the pressure-sensitive nerve endings, called the Pacini's corpuscles. Alternate hands to keep the motion constant.

**56**

The inner thighs are ultra-quivering to touch. They're also the home of the lymphatic system, which releases chemicals that cleanse the body of toxins. Which is why kneading a handful of the soft flesh in this area can create a pleasant buzzy state.

**57**

Using both hands, start at the hips and caress the flesh working your way toward the inner thighs. Now trace the same line with your mouth. Repeat this alternating sexy build-up until he can't take it any more (you'll know because he'll push your head toward a more central between-the-legs region).

# Toe the Line

Here are two caresses that'll get your feet wet.

Lather your hands with some massage oil and, applying pressure with your thumb, trace a line from the top of the big toe down into the valley between it and the second toe. Continue up the second toe and so on, repeating the movement all the way down to the little toe.

**59**

Give his tootsies a soaking by gently sucking the toes, from the big one down to the little one. Finish with a tongue swirl over the hyper-responsive in-step.

# Section Four

# Spicy Hot, Hot, Hot

You've tried different positions, various locations, and new hotspots in your bedroom play. Now it's time to turn up the heat and try a walk on the wild side. Here, for your pleasure, is a selection of just-this-side-of-kinky ways (no dog collars or whips included) to take your foreplay to the edge. Thrown into your repertoire, these moves will add spice, boost your connection and deliver some down-and-dirty instant gratification.

One note before you strip down: Never introduce something out-of-the-ordinary without a little build-up first. Make it sexy by waiting until you're both naked and heated (i.e., when your partner is more likely to let you have your wicked way) and whisper, "Wanna try something different?" Even if they don't go for what you have in mind, you'll find out what their definition of "kinky" is. Now use that knowledge for good… and go blow your mind.

# Hair Today, Gone Tomorrow

Experiment with better grooming.

**60**

While there are salons that will make you smooth as Sinatra, you can shave the hair off yourself. Think buzz cut, not bald. Remove it all and you'll soon find out why you have pubic hair: It prevents skin burns. Concentrate on the sides and the areas down below.

**61**

There are five basic options for taking it off. You'll need a mirror or a partner with a steady hand for all of them.

- **Shaving:** Condition your hair first (it makes removal easier) and use a sharp razor, scissors or an electric shaver to shape your hairline into whatever pattern you like.

- **Depilatories:** Spread the cream on thick, wait five to ten minutes and rinse. Watch out for clogged drains.

- **Waxing:** Put waxed strips where you want to take it off and – youch – strip! A good pick if you're considering a little S&M experimentation with your partner (you being the "M").

- **Brazilian Bikini:** A more intense version of waxing that also removes hair from the inner thighs, buttocks and sometimes the entire pubic region. Double youch!

- **Electrical or Laser Treatments:** You need a pro for this one as your hair will be removed permanently with special equipment. Not for those who change their mind easily!

Instead of a complete shave with a razor (which can leave an itch), trim each other using electric clippers. **Bonus:** The extra buzz can trigger an orgasm.

62

If he isn't sure about giving his forest a prune, tell him that the shorter the pubic hair, the bigger his organ looks.

63

# Watch and Learn

Whether it's viewing some raunchy porn action or watching your lover getting off, a little knowledge is a wonderful thing.

Don't act like you caught him cheating if you discover him in a self-embrace. You want a lover who's comfortable working his own pleasure. Here's why…

**64**

- According to studies, people who masturbate are more likely to get off when with someone else. So their self-fulfilment will make you seem like a better lover.

- Your lover is also more likely to be in the mood in two shakes. That's because all the action boosts hormone levels, especially testosterone and oestrogen, which primes a woman by producing wetness.

- If your partner knows how to work their own buttons, they can train you more easily (and teach you some cramp-relieving shortcuts).

Take one step beyond and let your lover watch as you get acquainted with yourself (or tag team each other).

**65**

Don't just watch: Do! Getting in on their act may make your lover feel more comfy about showing all in front of you. Try giving them your hand and asking them to guide it over their body, however feels good. Or ask to put your hand on top of theirs.

# 67

Make them feel like they're part of a threesome – while they self-service, stroke another bit of their body.

Watching porn can also give you some insider info to the opposite sex. But it will not produce the desired results (white-hot blinding lust) if your naughty video of choice features a seriously clueless bimbo, who keeps getting banged by big men out of the blue or lots of naked men and women sitting around talking. Pick a couple of friendly flicks (check out the user-friendly rating system at **www. goodvibrations.com** and **www.evesgarden.com**).

# Getting the Vibe

Get ready to swipe the batteries
out of your TV's remote control.

Some vibrators shake, rattle, roll and even lick. But if
you're shopping for the dream his-'n'-her machine,
opt for something that fits in the palm of your hand,
such as a finger vibrator, mini bullet or pocket rocket.
It'll produce the same power vibes as a mega version
without freaking out either of you over its size (see
tips 12 and 68 for resources).

**70**

Give him something to buzz about. Strap him into a vibrating cock ring (tips 12 and 68 tell you where to buy) and hold on tight for his orgasmic blast-off. If you really want to send him into the stratosphere, position the vibrator lower down behind his ball bearings.

**71**

Work the sides. The pulsing sensation from a vibrator can be too intense for direct contact on sensitive bits. Start at your outermost extremities, pushing down hard. Moving in tiny circles, work your way in, gradually letting up on the pressure so that by the time you reach the bull's eye, the vibrator is barely touching the skin.

Don't get lazy: It's not just that little guy by himself but the sexy combo of you and your battery-operated mate that sends your partner into seventh (or even eighth) heaven. Here are four ways to work together to get the best orgasmic results.

- Run the vibrator over your partner's nipples while you lick below.

- Team up down under – alternate using your mouth and your buzzing buddy.

- Make it feel like an orgy by working your other hand into the mix.

- Rub the vibrator along parts of their body that you don't usually think of as sexy and see how fast you revise your opinion.

**73**

Here are four things that are better than a vibrator.

- **Kissing.** Lips meeting, teeth-knocking, tongue -ashing kisses are the stuff that love is made of (check out tips one to nine for great suck-ups).

- **Using your tongue.** The two great things are that it's soft and wet. Your vibrator is not.

- **Nipple sucking.** Many woman (and men) can get off just from having their chest knobs kissed.

- **A warm body.** Sure, your Mr Buzz may be able to go all night and into next week without stopping, but will he cuddle you after?

# Adjust Your Thermostat

Playing with temperatures can make lukewarm lovemaking sizzle.

Adding heat to the right spots has a knock-on effect of literally raising your body's temperature, causing blood flow to increase, which in turn makes your skin more come-hither to touch. End result: You're screaming, "C'mon, baby, light my fire." Be warned – a little heat goes a long way. Here's how to get things smokin'.

- Blow. Warm breath on the skin raises its temperature. Head for less obvious thin-skinned spots like the earlobes, neck and inner thighs.

74

- Work up a slow burn by gently massaging a small blob of heat-activated lube (check out tips 12 and 68 for where to buy) all over his penis. The longer you rub, the warmer it gets.

- Sip some hot water, but don't swallow. Instead, carefully swallow him. The heated liquid will bring him to boiling point.

- Dribble warmed-up (finger-test the temperature first) honey, chocolate or syrup over their body and lick off.

**75**

Adding a frosty touch to your foreplay can actually make things hotter because it energizes your nerve cells. Here's how to add thrills with chills.

- Ice him. After working his body into a sweat, run an ice cube from his neck all the way down one side of his body, up the inside of his leg (but staying away from his heat stick), down the other side and back up.

- Crank the mercury back up to heatwave numbers by doing the above, but hold the ice cube in your hot little mouth this time.

- Fill a condom with water and freeze. Peel off and instant, presto, you have a dildo lolly to play with.

- Make an ice cream sundae out of their body. Don't forget the cherry on top.

76

Blow hot and cold. Done in succession, these two sensations pack a one-two wallop to your orgasms. The easiest way is to lick a small area and then blow hot air on the wet patch. Even better is to use booze because the alcohol evaporates more quickly than water, so it creates a cooler effect when you blow.

# Playing Rough

Think of these moves as tough love. Remember to establish a safe word before you start in case you want to put a stop to things mid-action.

78

Get hard on him. He's the stronger sex, so he can take it. Pinch his nipples (an often-overlooked nerve centre), scratch your nails down his back, massage his chest, knead his bottom, squeeze his boy parts. He'll get off on your girl-gone-wild manhandling.

A little love tap on the bottom can add some power to your foreplay. Remember that his bottom is not your boss's face, so use a light touch. First, prime the area with some rubbing. When you do finally smack, keep your hand relaxed and slightly cupped so it's more of a caress than a stinging slap. Run your other hand between his legs at the same time and you'll soon see what a naughty boy he can be.

You could invest in locks, Velcro or special ties, but go for a more soft-core approach that doesn't require too much preparation other than clean linen. Take turns wrapping each other in the bed sheet so the arms are pinned but the head, shoulders and lower legs uncovered. Now kiss every inch of exposed skin. The helpless sensation of only being able to receive pleasure can be very addictive.

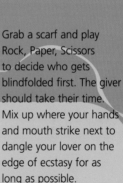

Grab a scarf and play Rock, Paper, Scissors to decide who gets blindfolded first. The giver should take their time. Mix up where your hands and mouth strike next to dangle your lover on the edge of ecstasy for as long as possible.

## Section Five

# Melt-down Moves

To really give your foreplay a blood-pumping jolt (and make the mattress springs squeak), you need to get out of your routine and strut your stuff into titilating new territory.

But that doesn't mean you should ditch what works. After all, those tried-and-true moves are the makings of orgasms. Nor must you risk arrest in a public place (unless you want to).

It does mean injecting a little of the unexpected into the proceedings, however. So if the last venture you made out of your safe zone was longer than a month ago, it's time to read through these melt-down moves and discover your hidden turn-ons.

# Mix It Up

Repetition is great for learning the multiplication table, but it doesn't do much for your sex life. According to an Archives of Sexual Behaviour study, just doing one thing differently can tally up your foreplay pleasure. Here are new ways to liven up your standard repertoire.

Learn the formula: If an area gets too much continual stimulation, it gets desensitized. Three minutes is enough to keep things interesting before moving on.

03:00 00

Here are four new techniques that will make him want to give you a round of applause (not to mention return the favour – tell him to study tips 84 to 85).

# 82

- Vary your type of touching: Switch from circles to side-to-side swipes.

- Polish his knob. Grease your hands with plenty of lube. Palm the head of his penis with one hand, pressing down and moving in tiny circles. Meanwhile, joggle the shaft with your other hand.

- Stop the action in the middle of a handjob and tickle the underside of his penis with your fingers or a feather.

- Lace your fingers together and wrap them around his piston. You can move up and down, twist back and forth or combine the two while squeezing to work him into a tailspin.

# 83

Three games for playing ball with him.

- Don't just grease up his bat. Squirt some lube between your hands and gently rub it all around his testicles.

- Wrestle his testicles into joyful submission by gently tugging on them.

- Get him to sit up and beg by using your finger to lightly scratch the underside of his balls.

Four fresh moves he can try on your clitoris. Be warned:
You may accidentally promise to become his love slave
after he performs these on you.

• Most men do
wrong by the clitoris because they
go for a heads-on rubdown, which can
actually be painful (probably not the sensation
you're hoping for). For more sati-sighing results, have
him gently play with the tip or rub a finger along the sides.

• Your clitoris is a very sensitive soul. Make sure it doesn't get
manhandled by having him switch-hit between rubbing, stroking,
licking and sucking, varying the amount of pressure he applies.

• You need lube, too. Even if you make your own juice, a spritz of
water-based lubricant on your nub will heighten sensation and
cut down on the friction that can rub you the wrong way.

• Getting him to lie perpendicular to your body
means he can stroke or lick you crosswise
rather than the usual
up and down.

Teach him to read your lips with these three lessons in love.

- Packed with nerve endings, the labia are so much more than a pitstop on the way to the vagina. Have him hold each one between his thumb and forefinger and massage it, working his way up and down.

- His finger is not a stand-in for his penis. So once he does gain entry, he shouldn't start jamming back and forth. Much more sexy is if he crooks his hands so that he can slip one finger in and wiggle it ever-so-slightly about while using his thumb to wag up and down your outer bits (if he's got long digits, he may even be able to reach your joy button).

- Get him to gently pull back your labia as if he's opening curtains so that your entire love region is exposed. He can now work his thumb and tongue over and under and all about.

Three nifty ways to become bosom buddies
(men have nipples, too).

- Lightly lick the outline of the nips
  in smaller and smaller circles until
  you have just the point in your
  mouth. Swirl with your tongue
  and reverse the sequence.

- Pucker your lips around
  the nipple and suck so
  that your mouth forms a
  seal. Ante up the pressure
  by inhaling and exhaling.

- Remind him that there is so
  much more to your breasts
  than the gumdrops on the
  top. Get him to caress and
  lick the sensitive top, bottom
  and sides of your breasts
  before coming in for a
  nipple landing.

86

# Moan Zones

Enter at your own orgasmic risk.

**GET INTO HIS ZONE:**

- Flirt with his fraenulum, the bundle of nerve endings just on the underside of the penis where the foreskin attaches to the head. When you're working his penis with your hand, squeeze a little extra pressure from your fingers directly on this spot with every downward stroke. Have a tissue handy for unexpected explosions.

- Hit his U note. The urethra is the tiny area of tissue above the opening (yes, it's the some spot where his pee comes). Press it lightly and he'll liquify.

- Walk his line. The raphe is the ridge that runs lengthways along the scrotum. Trace your fingers along it to the tip of his penis. Try not to fall off.

**PUT HIM ON YOUR TIME ZONE:**

• Have him give you the finger. This is the best move for pushing your G-spot (a soft swelling that lives halfway up the front wall of your vagina that will make you scream with joy when pressed). He should slide his thumb up about 2 in (5 cm) and press hard as if he were trying to make a thumbprint on the front of your vaginal wall.

• Say Aaaah! Studies show that merely finger stroking your anterior fornix zone (located on the front wall of the vagina between the G-Spot and the cervix) can juice you up and multiple orgasms.

88

**ZONE OUT TOGETHER:**

• Patch things up. The perineum (the passion patch of skin between your respective treasure chests and backsides) is made from the same sensitive tissues as your other sex organs. Rubbing a finger right there, light and fast, will make you both squirm.

• Get bummed. That tiny little hole is actually crammed with spine-tingling nerves. You don't have to go in deep; a well-lubed finger pressing around the outer regions is all it takes to cause a melt-down. If you do want to go in further, make sure your fingers and the entire area are clean and well-lubed.

89

# Double Play

Get twice as turned on by divvying up
your moves between two different spots.

You'll make him feel like he's part
of a lusty ménage-à-trois when
you work both of your hands on
different points of his body at the
same time. Keep one hand around
his love stick while using your other
hand to scratch his inner thighs,
balls or to stroke his bottom.

91

Work one hand between the legs while sucking on your lover's finger at the same time, using the same moves with your tongue as your digits are using down below. Your lover won't know if he's coming or going.

92

Get him to button you up by lightly tapping with his tongue or finger on the top of your clitoris while caressing the top of your bottom where the crease ends.

**93**

You'll go ga-ga when he slides one finger inside of you while gently rolling your love kernel between the thumb and forefinger of his other hand.

**94**

Give each other some skin. It's the largest sex organ on the body so the more you touch it, the better. While you're squeezing each other's other organs, rub your feet together and up and down each other's legs, push your bellies against each other and wriggle your pelvises. Get in touch wherever and however you can.

**95**

Lightly bite your lover's nipples (this goes for him, too) while touching down below. Expect sparks.

**96**

Turn his penis into his eleventh finger. Grasp it at the base and slowly rub it over your clitoris. At the same time, reach behind and work your fingers against the rim of each other's rear entries. Bliss off!

Get him to give you a full working over inside, outside and through the back. He begins with a sweet circular stroke to your love bud. Once you're feeling fine, he crooks his forefinger into a "come hither" position and slips it inside of you to tap lightly against the G-Spot. While tapping, he substitutes his tongue for the finger working your genital blossom. This frees up that hand to gently rotate around your back garden. Don't be surprised if you promise a BJ a day for the rest of his life in the heat of passion.

# The Big Bang

How to know when they're going to blow…
and what you can do about it.

**Two ways to get a cue:**

- Moans, gasps and cries of "Oh my God, I think I'm gonna come" are generally good indicators that you've got a good thing going.

- Someone starts issuing "Uh, a little to your left. Ooh, a little to the right. Higher – no, higher" instructions.

**Three signs he must ignore:**

98

- Your love buzzer goes into hiding. When she's close to climaxing, the clitoris retracts beneath the hood.

- You're not getting juicy. Lubrication depends on so many things – your hormones, your cycle, your diet. So how much motion lotion you're making is not a good indicator of how ready you are to rumble.

- You become very still. You shouldn't mention this too much because he gets jealous, but women are capable of coming again and again. So when you first freeze, chances are you're riding your first orgasmic wave.

# 99

Not ready to call an end to your play? Try these six tricks to get him to stay in the game for as long as you want.

- Add a chill – such as an ice cube or wet towel – against the small of his back to distract him long enough to regain control. Cold shower, anyone?

- To keep his tongue from getting tired, he should try sticking it out, closing his mouth around it and moving his lips and nose to work your bits.

- To give him a second wind, lay him down flat. This will stop the blood flow from springing his love gun back into firing stance.

- If he starts dribbling, let him go. He's reached the point of no return and risks straining or even tearing his urethra in his attempts to squeeze back the flow.

- If he's regularly trigger happy, help him put his safety lock on by holding the shaft of his penis in your hand, firmly squeezing for ten seconds and then releasing.

- Slip on a condom. A love glove helps keep him in check. A desensitizing gel may slow things down, but you risk transferring it and numbing your own happy regions.

Ready for the grand finale? Here are seven things you can do right this minute that guarantee orgasm. Hold on to your hat!

# 100

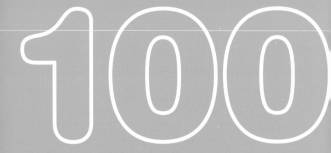

- **Give yourselves a hand.** If you need to seal the deal quickly, try mimicking your body's pre-orgasm movements. That means cupping his testicles in your hand and gently pressing up toward his body while you clench and release your PC (pubococcygeus) muscles (the same ones you use to control your pee flow).

• **Teach his fingers to figure skate.** Instead of working your clitoris in an up-and-down motion, have him trace around it as if he were drawing an "8" over and over and – mmm – over. By constantly varying the degrees of pressure between hard and soft, he'll soon put you into a layback spin.

• **Mix it up.** When your orgasms are stuck in a rut, shake things up by moving in slow motion or shifting things up to fifth gear.

• **Push his eject button.** Keeping a steady pressure on his prostate (see tip 87) will launch his load in seconds.

- **Get him to keep 'em coming.** Take a brief pause for intermission and then resume the action. But because you're bits are ultrasensitive, he should gradually ease off on the pressure after each body rush.

- **Hold your breath.** When you climax, you experience a toe-curling head rush. Multiply that by 1,000 by holding your breath for five seconds just as you start to

- **Have him multiply.** This doesn't mean he's going to keep on erupting. Orgasm is the moment when your pelvic muscles pleasurably contract at the peak of a sexual experience and similar in men and women. Ejaculation is a lower-spinal reflex that expels semen from the body. When you sense his fuse is about to blow, use the safety lock techniques in tip 99 to help him regain control. Then rapidly work him up to the brink again. With enough practice, he'll be captain of his penis, able to command it at will to orgasm without losing any of his erection-strengthening love juices.